FOREWORD

Welcome to the October 2013 edition of the Stability Operations Lessons Learned and Information Management System (SOLLIMS) Lessons Learned "Sampler" – **Key Enablers for Peacekeeping & Stability Operations.**

The general structure of the "Sampler" includes (1) an Introduction that provides an operational or doctrinal perspective for the content, (2) the Sampler **"Quick Look"** that provides a short description of the topics included within the Sampler and a link to the full text, (3) the primary, topic-focused Stability Operations (SO)-related Lesson Report, and (4) links to additional reports and other references that are either related to the "focus" topic or that address current, real-world, SO-related challenges.

This lessons-learned compendium contains just a sample – thus the title of "Sampler" – of the observations, insights, and lessons related to **Key Enablers for Peacekeeping & Stability Operations** available in the SOLLIMS data repository. These lessons are worth sharing with military commanders and their staffs, as well as with civilian practitioners having a Stability Operations-related mission / function – those currently deployed on stability operations, those planning to deploy, the institutional Army, policy-makers, and other international civilian and military leaders at the national and theater level.

Lesson Format. Each lesson is provided in the following standard format:

- Title/Topic
- Observation
- Discussion
- Recommendation
- Implications (optional)
- Event Description

The "Event Description" section provides context in that it identifies the source or event from which the lesson was developed. Occasionally you may also see a "Comments" section. This is used by the author to provide related information or additional personal perspective.

You will also note that a number is displayed in parentheses next to the title of each lesson. This number is hyper-linked to the actual lesson within the SOLLIMS database; click on the highlighted number to display the SOLLIMS data and to access any attachments (references, images, files) that are included with this lesson. Note, you must have an account and be logged into SOLLIMS in order to display the SOLLIMS data entry and access / download attachments.

If you have not registered on SOLLIMS, the links in the reports will take you to the login or the registration page. Take a brief moment to register for an account in order to take advantage of the many features of SOLLIMS and to access the Stability Operations-related products referenced in the report.

We encourage you to take the time to provide us with your perspective on any given lesson in this report or on the overall value of the "Sampler" as a reference for you and your unit/organization. By using the "Perspectives" text entry box that is found at the end of each lesson – seen when you open the lesson in your browser – you can enter your own personal comments on the lesson. We welcome your input, and we encourage you to become a regular contributor.

At PKSOI we continually strive to improve the services and products that we provide for the global stability operations community. We invite you to use our website at [**http://pksoi.army.mil**] and the many functions of the SOLLIMS online environment [**https://sollims.pksoi.org**] to help us identify issues and resolve problems. We welcome your comments and insights!

Ghazni Province, Afghanistan – Sergeant 1st Class Scott Shepro (U.S. Army) has the opportunity to meet with village elders during this combined Afghan-Coalition foot patrol. [Photo credit: Sergeant Mike MacLeod (U.S. Army), 8 May 2013.]

INTRODUCTION

Welcome to the October 2013 edition of the SOLLIMS Sampler! The focus for this edition is **Key Enablers for Peacekeeping and Stability Operations**.

> *"Bringing lasting peace and stability to regions devastated by violent conflict is a daunting and urgent task. Equally important is facilitating cooperation among the diverse institutions involved..."*
>
> *Guide for Participants in Peace, Stability, and Relief Operations,*
> **United States Institute of Peace (USIP)**

It is imperative that planners of peacekeeping and stability operations consider the full range of resources, systems, and tools that could be brought to bear to facilitate mission success for the forces involved. In this SOLLIMS Sampler, we present just a few of these "enablers" – specific resources, systems, and tools that have worked particularly well in support of recent and ongoing operations, including Operation Enduring Freedom (OEF) in Afghanistan and several peacekeeping operations in Africa. The "enablers" highlighted in this volume are:

- "Information gathering and analysis" mechanisms

- Civ-mil planning teams (i.e., Interagency planning teams)

- Strategic messaging / information operations

- Police units – with policewomen

- "Peace building" programs

- Governance capacity-building strategies

- Civilian Casualty (CIVCAS) prevention measures

This listing is not all-inclusive – by any means. However, it brings to light some relatively new developments / new organizations in peacekeeping and stability operations – namely, all-female Formed Police Units (FPUs) and Civilian Casualty Tracking Cells (CCTCs). It also resurrects and revalidates a number of "old and proven" systems – namely, "information gathering and analysis," civ-mil planning, and strategic messaging / information operations. In some cases, these "old and proven" systems were effectively employed with a new twist in design or execution, as discussed in the **Lesson Report**. Additionally, this listing identifies two "enablers" that probably merit much greater attention / resourcing when planning and executing future operations – namely, "peace building" programs and governance capacity-building strategies – in order to better address societal grievances, build legitimacy, and expediently place the Host Nation in the lead.

Key take-aways are captured in the **Conclusion** paragraph.

Key Enablers for Peacekeeping & Stability Operations

Table of Contents

"QUICK LOOK"

Click on [Read More ...] to go to full lesson.

- It is imperative that forces deployed on stability operations have sufficient resources for "information gathering and analysis" throughout the force structure – and especially at lower levels. [Read More ...]

- At U.S. Embassy Kabul, a small interagency (IA) team of planners, assessors, and action officers in the Political-Military Affairs section has helped orient civ-mil relations toward the main goal of building capacity... [Read More ...]

- Military Information Support Operations (MISO) contributed to the success of operations conducted by USAFRICOM and NATO against the Ghadafi regime in Libya in 2011... [Read More ...]

- All-female Formed Police Units (FPUs) serving on UN peacekeeping missions in Liberia and the Democratic Republic of the Congo (DRC) have effectively improved security in those post-conflict environments. [Read More ...]

- In the immediate aftermath of the December 2007 elections in Kenya ... The actions of the Concerned Citizens for Peace (CCP) during this crisis of emergent/ spiraling violence is a tremendous example of utilizing civil society peace building capacity, mobilizing a larger constituency on short notice, incorporating multi-sector and multi-level actions, and teaming with a parallel formal mediation effort. [Read More ...]

- With an eye toward transition, the United Nations Mission in Liberia (UNMIL) shifted the role of the UN peacekeeping force (the UNMIL force) in early 2008 from "leading" the delivery of services (security, reconstruction, social services, etc.) to "enabling" the Government of Liberia to take lead. [Read More ...]

- The Kandahar City-District Stabilization Team (KC-DST), in close coordination with Combined Task Force (CTF) Lancer, reversed the trend of "excessive ISAF support to Kandahar City officials" and implemented a new strategy (disengagement strategy) to put "Afghans in the lead." [Read More ...]

- During Operation Enduring Freedom (OEF) in Afghanistan, the tracking and analysis of civilian casualties, along with command emphasis on civilian casualty (CIVCAS) prevention led to a significant decrease in civilian casualties. [Read More ...]

U.S. Army Peacekeeping and Stability Operations Institute
U.S. Army War College
22 Ashburn Drive, Upton Hall
Carlisle Barracks, PA 17013

22 October 2013

SUBJECT: Key Enablers for Peacekeeping & Stability Operations

1. GENERAL

In the course of recent / ongoing operations in Afghanistan, the Democratic Republic of the Congo (DRC), Kenya, Liberia, Libya, and Sierra Leone, a number of key "enablers" have significantly contributed to mission accomplishment.   In most cases, these "enablers" were developed / instituted to address a specific need or shortfall, and they rather quickly made a positive operational impact for the forces involved. Granted, no two operations are ever alike, however, the key "enablers" covered in this report are nonetheless offered as "food for thought" for planners and practitioners of future peacekeeping and stability operations.

2. LESSONS

a. TOPIC. Resources for Information Gathering and Analysis (1194)

Observation.

It is imperative that forces deployed on stability operations have sufficient resources for "information gathering and analysis" throughout the force structure – and especially at lower levels.

Discussion.

Stability operations in Afghanistan and multiple peacekeeping operations in Africa have shown the importance of placing robust information gathering elements at the lower levels, supported by information centers at the operational level and by "reachback" centers at the strategic level.

Operating Enduring Freedom (OEF) – Afghanistan: In mid-2010, after years of inadequate situational awareness, the International Security Assistance Force (ISAF) senior intelligence officer called for a "sea change" in intelligence operations. Deficiencies stemmed from:

- Traditional intelligence systems in Afghanistan were seen as failing the needs of senior U.S. decision-makers. Those systems emphasized threat-focused ("red") information and paid little attention to population-focused "white" information (about communities, tribes, groups, leaders, etc.). Stability

Operations Information Centers were called for and stood-up at the operational level to support this requirement. Additional analysts were needed at these centers and at lower level units. (Reference 1)

- Military commanders and local governmental administrators needed a means to understand the social systems of the various communities and tribes, and also a way to understand and predict how military activities would affect those social systems. (Reference 2)

- There was a need to "get dirty" and go down to village level, address tribal, clan, even family level concerns. With no formal model/system in place, "valleyism" was suggested – i.e., gaining an understanding of the political, economical, and cultural drivers within each "valley" and local region. There was a need for intelligence and information centers within CONUS to provide reach-back support and help determine how to get "village" issues connected to the national system. (References 3 and 4)

- "The best and most useful information was coming from the bottom and not from the top." (Reference 5)

- According to a Joint Doctrine Bulletin, "the volume and diversity of information means that the Provincial Reconstruction Team (PRT) needed an intelligence section of sufficient size and quality able to provide the commander with good situational awareness after the information has been processed and analyzed" – yet the PRT intelligence section's strength was typically one person. (References 6 and 7)

- An example of a hard lesson learned was the debacle in Bala Morghab, Badghis Province: "Pay attention to the intelligence effort. Intelligence should drive/influence operations. Indicators and actual incidents of insurgent activity in and around Bala Morghab were repeatedly reported, yet they were ignored – with dire consequences."   17 killed, 20 wounded, 24 captured. (Reference 8)

Multinational Peacekeeping Operations in Africa:

- In United Nations (UN) peacekeeping operations in Sierra Leone in early 2000, the UN Mission in Sierra Leone (UNAMSIL) nearly collapsed when the rebel Revolutionary United Front (RUF) kidnapped approximately 500 peacekeepers. With no knowledge of the terrain and unfamiliar with the rebels' military tactics, type of equipment, and intentions, UN troops were completely taken by surprise. After this crisis, UNAMSIL quickly moved to address this deficiency by creating a Military Information Cell at the force headquarters. The Military Information Cell soon established a broad network of information gathering assets/ sources – using troop contingents, military observers, civilian personnel, and public information officers deployed all around the country to gather relevant information. The Military Information Cell was integrated into the

Joint Operations Center of the mission, which became the central point of contact for information exchanges, reporting, and analysis. (Reference 9)

- In the Africa Center for Strategic Studies research paper "Enhancing Civilian Protection in Peace Operations in Africa," Paul D. Williams provides detailed illustrations of peacekeeping and civilian protection problems that took place during operations in Rwanda (1993-1994), the Democratic Republic of the Congo (DRC) (2001-2010), and Sudan (2004-2010), caused in part by the lack of intelligence resources/personnel. He recommends: "Invest in intelligence capabilities. Peacekeeping organizations need to develop efficient forms of intelligence-gathering. The protection of civilians cannot be accomplished without gathering appropriate intelligence on the operating environment and conducting detailed threat analysis." (Reference 10)

- In the case of the UN's Mission in the Democratic Republic of the Congo (MONUC), significant improvements were made through the use of <u>Joint Protection Teams</u>. These teams were comprised of civil affairs, human rights, and child protection personnel, and were supported by interpreters. Over 80 such teams were positioned at MONUC's bases in North Kivu beginning in 2010. Deployed to the field for days at a time, these teams worked to gain an understanding of conflict dynamics, created links between MONUC and the local population, collected data on local environments, and provided early warning of perceived/assessed threats. They provided a steady flow of reliable information in support of MONUC's planning and operations. (Reference 11)

- In April 2013, speakers at the Challenges Forum Workshop in Entebbe, Uganda, described recent experiences by several United Nations missions to correct and strengthen information gathering and analysis. It was suggested that the challenge for information gathering often begins with flaws in planning and priority setting for missions. The information gathering cycle should be driven through targeted priority information requirements (PIR), yet this is not necessarily a tool understood or used by many senior leaders. In many missions, personnel working in Joint Mission Analysis Centers (JMACs) or Joint Operations Centers (JOCs) have had to work extremely hard with senior managers to elicit actionable PIRs (or "what you need to know?") from the mission leadership to focus information gathering efforts. (Reference 12)

Success Stories / Model Approaches:

<u>1st Battalion, 5th Marines in Helmund Province (Afghanistan).</u> The battalion established mini-intelligence shops at lower/company levels. Every night, the battalion intelligence section hosted "fireside chats," during which time subordinate analysts radioed in from remote positions – relaying information gained over the past 24 hours. Information encompassed patrol debriefings, notes of officers who had met with local leaders, observations of civil affairs officers, and human intelligence reports. At the end of the "fireside chats," the

battalion intelligence officer assigned subordinates new Intelligence Requirements (IR) for the next day's activities. The focus of those IR started with conditions of roads, bridges, mosques, markets, wells, and key terrain. It gradually shifted to local leaders and residents and their perceptions. It then shifted further to what were called "anchor points" – local grievances and local personalities, who/which, if skillfully exploited, could drive a wedge between the greater population and the insurgents. Identifying and addressing the "anchor points" (or "local irritants') was instrumental to the battalion gaining success on stability operations. (Reference 1)

<u>1st Squadron, 91st Cavalry Regiment in Nuristan and Kunar Provinces (Afghanistan).</u> The intelligence shop devoted the bulk of its resources to understanding the social relationships, economic disputes, and religious and tribal leadership throughout the local communities. Using this information, the squadron worked to strengthen traditional power structures supported by elders, and deflated local insurgent activity. Whereas more than 30 American and Afghan soldiers had been killed in the five months prior to the squadron's tour of duty in Nuristan and Kunar provinces, only three deaths occurred over the next 12 months throughout those areas. Relentless engagement with local elders, leaders, and powerbrokers, and pulsing them on issues and irritants, was absolutely critical to success. (Reference 1)

<u>Human Terrain System (HTS) – supporting OIF and OEF.</u> In contrast to the work of intelligence assets/organizations (which were collecting and analyzing threat-focused information), human terrain teams (HTTs) were deployed to conduct "social science" research and gain insights on local population groups – to better enable planning activities and decision-making. The HTTs placed their emphasis on operationally relevant aspects of local cultures; on the various ethno-religious, tribal, and other divisions within society and their sentiments; and, on the multiple interests of population groups and leaders. The HTS Reachback Research Center (composed of cells at Fort Leavenworth, Kansas and at Newport News, Virginia) provided invaluable support to deployed forces – one cell supporting the HTTs in Iraq, and the other supporting the HTTs in Afghanistan. (Reference 4)

<u>Joint Special Operations Task Force-Philippines (JSOTF-P).</u> U.S. Army Military Information Support (MIST) teams and Civil Affairs (CA) teams were integrated with Armed Forces of the Philippines (AFP) units, predominantly at the tactical level. The MIST teams focused their efforts on radio messaging, atmospherics analysis (to gain insights on the thoughts and concerns of the people, especially about the government and its security forces), and on measures of effectiveness. The CA teams concentrated their actions on building AFP capacity to support the needs of local communities. As a result of these combined efforts, not only did JSOTF-P and the AFP gain far greater situational awareness, but also the AFP developed CA assets capable of planning,

resourcing, and conducting civic-action programs for the benefit of local communities – increasing support to the AFP. (Reference 13)

Recommendation.

1. Establish robust "information gathering and analysis" mechanisms – focused on the population – to provide forces/commanders of peacekeeping and stability operations with a comprehensive understanding of the operating environment. Models for consideration are highlighted in red in the Discussion section above.

2. Information collected at the ground level – from patrols, CA teams, force protection teams, MIST teams, human terrain teams, reconstruction teams, key leader engagements, etc. – should be given the greatest attention in peacekeeping and stability operations/environments. The preponderance of information and intelligence resources should be focused at this level, with sufficient analysts deployed at this level to manage PIR, IR, collection activities, de-briefings, analysis, and dissemination. Although "tactical" in nature, this information is absolutely vital to the production of accurate "operational" and "strategic" intelligence. (Reference 1)

Event Description.

This lesson is based on the following **REFERENCES:**

(1) "Afghanistan: Making Intelligence Relevant," SOLLIMS Lesson 680, 25 October 2010.

(2) "Planning Considerations for Military-Political Engagement in Afghanistan," SOLLIMS Lesson 669, 23 August 2010.

(3) "Defining, or Re-defining, the Role of Strategic Intelligence during Stability Operations," SOLLIMS Lesson 753, 17 June 2011.

(4) "Improved Situational Awareness from Human Terrain Teams," SOLLIMS Lesson 776, 2 February 2012.

(5) "Intelligence Sharing," SOLLIMS Lesson 602, 4 March 2011.

(6) "Information Management in Provincial Reconstruction Teams," SOLLIMS Lesson 448, 5 August 2009.

(7) "BCT-PRT 'Unity of Effort' Reference Guide," PKSOI, September 2011.

(8) "Failure of the Top-Down Approach in Afghanistan," SOLLIMS Lesson 775, 28 December 2011.

(9) "Lessons Learned from United Nations Peacekeeping Experiences in Sierra Leone," Peace-keeping Best Practices Unit, UN Department of Peacekeeping Operations, September 2003.

(10) "Enhancing Civilian Protection in Peace Operations: Insights from Africa," Paul D. Williams, Africa Center for Strategic Studies," September 2010.

(11) "Information Gathering, Intelligence, and Threat Analysis for Civilian Protection," SOLLIMS Lesson 699, 15 March 2011.

(12) "The Art of the Possible: Peace Operations under New Conditions," Challenges Forum Workshop Report, 29-30 April 2013.

(13) "Light Footprint and Whole-of-Government Approach – The Southern Philippines," SOLLIMS Lesson 911, 24 September 2012.

Comments.

THIS INFORMATION MAY BE OF INTEREST TO:

- Department of the Army – Deputy Chief of Staff, G-2, G-3/5/7

- Department of Defense – Joint Chiefs of Staff, J-2, J-3, J-5, J-7

- United Nations – Department of Peacekeeping Operations (UNDPKO)

Return to "Quick Look"

b. TOPIC. Embassy Planning in Afghanistan and Beyond (873)

Observation.

At U.S. Embassy Kabul, a small interagency (IA) team of planners, assessors, and action officers in the Political-Military Affairs (Pol-Mil) section has helped orient civ-mil relations toward the main goal of building capacity for the Afghan government and its society. This IA team – the Civ-Mil Plans and Assessments Sub-Section (CMPASS) – helps guide the complex civ-mil activities in Afghanistan – mainly by ensuring that the distinct perspectives and approaches of civilian agencies and military forces are closely coordinated – to mutually reinforce one another.

Discussion.

In 2009, the U.S. Embassy Kabul established CMPASS as a new Civ-Mil Plans office (J5) alongside the existing Pol-Mil Operations office (J3) and placed them both under one J3/J5 Director (Mr. Philip Kosnett). The CMPASS team was originally composed of five persons, but grew to seven personnel by mid-2011: four State Department planning officers from the Bureau of Conflict and Stabilization Operations, two additional State Department planners, and one U.S. Army field grade officer. The mission assigned to CMPASS was: to coordinate civ-mil actions among the Embassy, the International Security Assistance Force (ISAF), U.S. Forces Afghanistan (USFOR-A), and Afghan partners, and to provide planning and assessment support throughout the U.S. Mission.

To accomplish its mission, to help set and disseminate theater guidance, and to maximize the alignment of U.S., Afghan, and coalition activities, CMPASS works off of the Integrated Civilian-Military Campaign Plan. CMPASS routinely teams with the Embassy's Interagency Provincial Affairs (IPA) office, whose primary responsibility is to coordinate civ-mil actions between Kabul and the field. Additionally, CMPASS frequently collaborates with the U.S. Agency for International Development (USAID), notably its Stabilization Unit in Kabul and its military liaisons from both Combined Forces Special Operations Component Command and the ISAF Joint Command (IJC). Through working/collaborating with these offices, CMPASS is able to help prioritize strategic and operational objectives, synchronize civ-mil activities across time and space, agree upon ways to measure progress, and build flexibility and room for adaptation into civ-mil efforts.

CMPASS helps operationalize civ-mil integration first and foremost through its participation in the National Level Working Groups (NLWGs), which are civ-mil problem-solving teams structured around subject areas that address governance, elections, rule of law, anti-corruption, population security, reintegration, agriculture, infrastructure, borders, economic development, counter-narcotics, illicit finance, gender policy, and information initiatives. CMPASS serves as the Embassy's coordinating body for these working groups, and it helps to prepare agenda items and read-ahead packets for meetings between the Chief of Mission and ISAF Commander. CMPASS members also help to identify cross-cutting issues that require special consideration and additional coordination to achieve desired effects.

CMPASS has also served as the Embassy lead for preparing assessments that help define and measure progress in Afghanistan. In conjunction with State and USAID officials in Washington, CMPASS prepares quarterly assessments for the National Security Council, which the national security staff uses to evaluate the impact of its strategy and to prepare briefings for Congress. In this effort, CMPASS works closely with the Afghan Assessments Group at ISAF Headquarters and with the assessments group at ISAF Joint Command (IJC). CMPASS' assessments have addressed topics such as Afghan ministerial budget execution, anti-corruption and counter-narcotics measures, and progress on sub-national governance, private investment, and international donor coordination.

Some of the most important synchronization exercises for CMPASS have been intense interagency reviews of U.S. civ-mil efforts in Afghanistan called "Rehearsal of Concept (ROC) drills." These civ-mil ROC drills have been co-hosted by U.S. Embassy Kabul, U.S. Forces-Afghanistan, U.S. Central

Command, and the Office of the Special Representative for Afghanistan and Pakistan. These sessions have routinely included senior participants from the Embassy, USAID, ISAF, the Afghan ministries, the Afghan Supreme Court, and ambassadors and senior officials the European Union, the United Nations, and 11 other embassies. In preparing for and executing these senior-level events, CMPASS organized and facilitated the interagency coordination within the Embassy. As a result of these ROC drills, civ-mil planning and resource requirements have been better synchronized – between U.S., international, and host nation partners – along various lines of effort, including security, governance, agriculture, justice, economic development, anti-corruption, counter-narcotics, and border issues.

Recommendation.

1. Within any given U.S. embassy, establish and empower a planning team (like CMPASS) to focus on ensuring that the yearly State Department and USAID mission strategic plan informs the activities of the mission. This planning team could help facilitate periodic assessments with the ambassador to measure progress on the goals in the strategic plan and propose courses of action to address gaps or deficiencies. This planning team could also help organize periodic civ-mil ROC drills.

2. For civ-mil planning and training events, when numbers of U.S. Government Agency civilian personnel may be limited, the Agencies should coordinate with the military to identify the key times during the planning cycle that require critical civilian expertise, and then participate at those junctures with the right people.

3. Those involved in the complex business of planning stability operations should come to recognize the critical importance of building personal relationships. Planning is likely to improve when civilians and service members take time to get to know one another, understand the constraints that others are working under, and learn what is motivating them to work on the plan/operation.

Implication

If an embassy does not establish and empower a planning team (like CMPASS) to focus the activities of the mission on its yearly strategic plan, then execution of mission activities might prove to be disjointed or incomplete, and periodic assessments on progress toward goals might be absent or lacking.

Event Description.

This lesson is based on the article "Navigating Civil-Military Relations in Kabul," by Maria J. Stephan, InterAgency Journal, Vol. 3, Issue 1, Winter 2012.

Return to "Quick Look"

c. <u>TOPIC</u>. Military Information Support Operations (MISO) in Libya (<u>1255</u>)

Observation.

Military Information Support Operations (<u>MISO</u>) contributed to the success of operations conducted by USAFRICOM and NATO against the Ghadafi regime in Libya in 2011; however, personnel issues and information-sharing constraints hindered planning, coordination, and synchronization of MISO activities.

Discussion.

In February 2011, a small MISO Support Element (MSE) and <u>Commando Solo</u> – an aerial platform for broadcast media/messaging – deployed to Europe to support the non-combatant evacuation operation of third country nationals out of Libya. Over the course of the next eight months, however, their work expanded to include disseminating messages in support of humanitarian assistance, law of land warfare, non-interference, and the Protection of Civilians (PoC). The MSE and Commando Solo disseminated more than 50 messages throughout the 12 days of lethal activity during Operation Odyssey Dawn (21 March – 1 April 2011), and an additional 200 messages during the seven months of Operation Unified Protector (1 April - 31 October 2011).

On several occasions, owing to the effects of MISO, the Combined Joint Task Force (CJTF) was able to gain the attention of the Ghadafi regime and its supporters – causing them to expend time and energy responding to MISO messaging. The Ghadafi regime/supporters resorted to actions such as developing press releases, radio messages, and website postings in direct response to the MISO messages, in an effort to contradict them and to avoid losing supporters. Most significantly, a correlative relationship can be shown between Commando Solo messaging and the fall of certain regime strongholds, namely: Misratah, Tripoli, Sirte, and Bani Walide. Each of these cities was deliberately targeted by Commando Solo messaging, in conjunction with CJTF lethal activities. As a result, Transitional National Council Forces (the forces that were fighting against the Ghadafi regime) were not only able to capture these cities, but in some cases, they did so with very little regime opposition.

Although MISO contributed to the success of the Libyan campaign, the following personnel-related issues and information-sharing constraints hindered MISO operations:

   1) As the Libyan crisis situation was evolving, the <u>6th Military Information Support Operations Battalion</u> identified the need to send a unit representative to

USAFRICOM to contribute to its ongoing planning efforts. The battalion generated an order and deployed a MISO planner to USAFRICOM without an approved Request For Forces (RFF). This battalion-driven (bottom-up) process was fairly time-consuming and was not fast enough, nor comprehensive enough, to get MISO assets fully integrated into USAFRICOM's Joint Planning Team, Targeting Cell, and Humanitarian Working Group during the planning period. The one MISO planner was able to ensure that 11 MISO messages were broadcast on the first day that the JTF conducted a lethal attack/bombing mission. However, had the MISO battalion been able to deploy additional planners or liaison officers to USAFRICOM early during the planning period, then the initial series of MISO messages would have been much more comprehensive and better synchronized within the overall campaign plan to help achieve desired effects.

2) When the center of U.S. operations shifted from USAFRICOM to NATO's CJTF headquarters at Joint Forces Command Naples, two MISO personnel deployed to the CJTF and worked within its Joint Effects Management Cell (JEMC). These two personnel were fully qualified in MISO/PSYOP, but they did not possess Electronic Warfare (EW) expertise/qualification. The CJTF's EW officer was from Spain. Relevant intelligence (Commando Solo/MISO-related) that could have supported EW efforts was classified "Five Eyes," which meant that the Spanish EW officer could not have access to it, and he therefore could not coordinate and synchronize the information/frequencies needed. (Note: "Five Eyes" information was releasable to only Australia, Canada, New Zealand, United States, and Great Britain.) Since the U.S. MISO personnel did not have expertise/background in the EW specialty, they were not in a position to overcome the problem caused by the information-sharing constraint.

3) Joint Forces Command Naples had an authorization for a U.S. field grade PSYOP officer; however, that billet was unfilled and there was no U.S. PSYOP officer on station. As the Libyan crisis evolved, and as the transition from USAFRICOM to the NATO CJTF took place, that billet remained unfilled. The PSYOP Chief within the CJTF JEMC was an Italian PSYOP officer. Like the Spanish EW officer, he was handicapped by the information-sharing (classification) constraint, and he could not be "read on" to the capabilities of Commando Solo. The two U.S. MISO/PSYOP personnel (one captain, one NCO) who deployed to the JEMC could not coordinate with the Italian PYSOP Chief (a major) because of the classification level, yet they were able to go above him and coordinate actions with the JEMC Chief (a British major). Had there been a U.S. field grade officer on site, filling the authorized Joint billet, this awkward situation would not have emerged. Moreover, he could have been working the crisis planning actions from the outset.

Recommendation.

1. Continue to utilize MISO in support of stability operations – to help influence the attitudes/behaviors of the local populace in support of U.S./coalition operations, and to affect/impact the decision-making of opposition leaders/ groups/supporters.

2. Combatant Commanders should request MISO and Commando Solo assets early on during crisis/contingency planning – and incorporate these personnel into appropriate staffs/teams such as the Joint Planning Team, Targeting Cell, and Humanitarian Working Group.

3. The U.S. Army should afford EW and Deception training opportunities for MISO/PSYOP officers and non-commissioned officers, allowing them to become holistic practitioners of information operations (IO).

4. The U.S. Army should endeavor to fill Joint MISO/PSYOP billets, such as the one at Joint Forces Command Naples. When there is an unfilled billet at a Joint or Combatant Command during a crisis/contingency planning situation, the U.S. Army should quickly fill the void with a temporary fill.

5. Department of Defense/Combatant Commanders should consider making exceptions to information-sharing constraints (classification and releasability determinations) to support planning and conduct of operations. For example, expanding releasability of "Five Eyes" to NATO members to support a NATO operation.

Implications

If the aforementioned issues and recommendations are not addressed, then IO effects will not be maximized during the course of future operations/campaigns, due to deficiencies in planning, coordination, and synchronization.

Event Description.

This lesson is based on the article "Military Information Support to Contingency Operations in Libya," by Captain Geoffrey Childs, Special Warfare magazine, Volume 26, Issue 1, January - March 2013.

Comments

Related references and links:

(1) 6th Military Information Support Operations Battalion, Military.com.

(2) 4th Military Information Support Operations Group, Military.com.

(3) EC-130J Commando Solo III, Military.com.

(4) Joint Publication 3-13.2, Military Information Support Operations, with Change 1, Joint Chiefs of Staff, 20 December 2011.

(5) Operation Odyssey Dawn (OOD) and Operation Unified Protector (OUP) document collection, SOLLIMS USAFRICOM portal, Special Reports and Papers.

(6) Strategic Lesson Number 11: Strategic Messaging by Intervening Forces during Stability Operations, Dan French and Jared Edgerton, 30 July 2012.

Return to
"Quick Look"

d. **TOPIC. All-Female Formed Police Units (1257)**

Observation.

All-female Formed Police Units (FPUs) serving on UN peacekeeping missions in Liberia and the Democratic Republic of the Congo (DRC) have effectively improved security in those post-conflict environments. Moreover, they have proven to be an excellent asset for community-level peace building, as well as a major source of inspiration for women and girls.

Discussion.

In January 2007, India deployed a contingent of 103 policewomen to the United Nations Mission in Liberia (UNMIL). They provided the core of the first all-female Formed Police Unit (FPU) to ever serve on a United Nations peacekeeping operation. Initially 22 male staff personnel supported the FPU, but after several months, the organization was turned into an all-female FPU. Since then, there have been successive contingents of all-female FPUs in UNMIL, contributed by India.

The original tasks of the all-female FPU consisted of guarding the president's office, providing security at various public events having high-profile leaders in attendance, carrying out night patrols with members of the Liberian National Police (LNP) in and around the capital (Monrovia), and conducting riot control when needed. With each rotation, the FPU's roles expanded beyond the mandated tasks – to include supporting a wide range of community-focused programs, with particular emphasis on those involving Liberian women and girls. For example, the all-female FPUs conducted community summer camps, in which they taught self-defense, first aid, and classical Indian dance for Liberian girls.

Several researchers have indicated that the time and energy that female peacekeepers expended on interacting and communicating with the local community had an amazing influence. It was reported that when the all-female FPUs noticed decreasing attendance in various community programs, they made a concerted effort to approach both men and women, seeking to understand the reasons for their absenteeism or their withdrawal from certain activities. This approach resulted in a detailed understanding of the concerns, needs, and prevalent challenges of the community, which in turn facilitated the improvement of community programs, greater participation by community members, and significant strides in peace building to overcome friction and grievances.

Of note, in the areas where all-female FPUs operated, it was reported that sexual abuse and exploitation of women dropped sharply. Reports also showed an increase in the number of girls remaining in, and completing, primary school in those areas. Additionally, an increase in female recruitment in the LNP was ascribed to the all-female FPU, which is said to have inspired women to take on non-traditional roles – such as the security profession.

Overall, the presence of the Indian all-female FPU has led to enhanced physical safety and security in Monrovia and surrounding districts. Support from the Government of Liberia was contributory to the all-female FPU's success, as the Government not only supported the activities of the FPU, but also created awareness of its activities among the local populace. By increasing the FPU's visibility at public events and drawing attention to its presence in the community, security continued to improve.

In November 2011, Bangladesh deployed an all-female FPU to the United Nations Organization Stabilization Mission in the Democratic Republic of the Congo (MONUSCO). This first all-female FPU from Bangladesh began its work at a crucial point in time for the DRC, needing to establish security in a tense environment plagued by the violence surrounding the presidential and national legislative elections of 2011. The all-female FPU not only performed its tasks successfully, it also proved instrumental in saving many civilian lives during one period of heavy fighting in Kinshasa. Based on the FPU's success, Bangladesh replaced this unit with another 125-member all-female FPU in February 2013, and Bangladesh has committed to subsequent rotations as well.

The tasks of MONUSCO's all-female FPU have included: crowd control, the protection of the UN staff and facilities, and escorting UN personnel into various areas deemed insecure. In addition to these security tasks, the all-female FPU has worked to support various programs and events within the communities it has served. For instance, the Commander of the second FPU contingent, Shirin Jahan Akter, arranged to have the FPU participate in the International Women's Day event held in Kinshasa on 8 March 2013, where it provided a demonstration of martial art skills under the theme "Rise up Women, Awaken Your Power."

Such activities by the all-female FPU have had a significant positive impact on Congolese society at large, and its women in particular.

Recommendation.

1. The UN should continue the approach of sending all-female FPUs on select peacekeeping operations. This should be done on a case-by-case basis, depending on the UN's assessment of the given host nation environment and the willingness of contributing countries to deploy such units. In certain environments, all-female FPUs may be able to serve as key role models for host nation women and girls.

2. The UN and other organizations/coalitions engaged in peacekeeping operations should consider the benefits of having their deployed police/security forces engage in community peace building programs and activities.

Implications.

If the UN does not pursue the option of deploying all-female FPUs on appropriate missions, then an opportunity to provide role models for women and girls of the host nation by way of a cohesive, professional security organization may be lost. Also, the failure to couple "peacekeeping/stability operations" with "peace building activities" may translate to achieving only short-term security gains — without resolving long-standing grievances, maximizing participation/inclusivity, and potentially achieving long-term stability/peace.

Event Description.

This lesson is based on the article "Women in Peacekeeping: The Emergence of the All-Female Uniformed Units in UNMIL and MONUSCO," by Catherine A. Onekalit, in Conflict Trends, July 2013, published by ACCORD. ACCORD's website: http://www.accord.org.za.

Comments

Related references:

> (1) Female Participation in Formed Police Units: A Report on the Integration of Women in Formed Police Units of Peacekeeping Operations, by Charlotte Anderholt, PKSOI Paper, September 2012.

> (2) Gender Mainstreaming in Peacekeeping Operations Liberia 2003-2009: Best Practices Report, published by United Nations Mission in Liberia (UNMIL), in cooperation with Kofi Annan International Peacekeeping Training Centre (KAIPTC) and German Development Cooperation, September 2010.

(3) <u>Gender-Sensitive Police Reform in Post-Conflict Societies</u>, published by <u>UN Women</u>, 15 October 2012.

(4) <u>UN Police Peacekeeping</u>, presented by Damien Carrick, RN Law Report on <u>abc.net.au</u>, 21 July 2009.

(5) <u>Mindanao Peacebuilding Institute and Creating Peace through Grassroots Leadership</u>, by Kevin Doyle, SOLLIMS Lesson 1191, 17 June 2013.

Return to "Quick Look"

e. <u>TOPIC</u>. Civil Society Capacity and Action for Peace Building – Kenya (<u>702</u>)

Observation.

In the immediate aftermath of the December 2007 elections in Kenya, violent clashes broke out that threatened the very existence of the country. Besides the successful formal mediation efforts by the former United Nations Secretary-General Kofi Annan, an equally impressive "civil society response" – based on previously developed civil society peace building capacity – was absolutely critical to bringing about peace to this country in chaos. The actions of the Concerned Citizens for Peace (CCP) during this crisis of emergent/spiraling violence is a tremendous example of utilizing civil society peace building capacity, mobilizing a larger constituency on short notice, incorporating multi-sector and multi-level actions, and teaming with a parallel formal mediation effort.

Discussion.

Politically instigated ethnic clashes had been a well-known source of violent conflict in Kenya prior to the elections of December 2007. Ruthless politicians/ candidates had often utilized youth militia groups to carry out violent attacks on communities they perceived to be in opposition to their political agendas.

In December 2007, national presidential and parliamentary elections were held in Kenya. Mwai Kibaki and Raila Odinga were the two leading presidential candidates. In the months and weeks leading up to voting day, opinion polls favored Odinga and his party. Early voting results on 27 December indicated that Odinga had built a comfortable lead. However, this lead gradually eroded, and, as election day passed and two more days passed without a presidential winner being declared, tensions and anxiety among Kenyans gave way to many violent clashes and incidents. Finally, on 30 December, the Electoral Commission of Kenya announced that Kibaki had actually won. With this announcement, Kenya exploded into unprecedented and widespread violence/conflict. 1,300 people lost their lives, and more than 500,000 people were displaced.

Within 24 hours of the 30 December announcement, in the midst of the spiraling violence, a new civil society group called Concerned Citizens for Peace (CCP) was launched by five prominent Kenyan civil society peace workers and mediators, including two retired general officers. The group's formation was widely announced to the public. Among the CCP's five core leaders was Ms. Dekha Ibrahim Abdi, well known as a founding member of the Wajir Peace and Development Committee. By way of background, Ms. Abdi had worked with a number of women back in the 1993-95 timeframe to address a cycle of violence in the Wajir district of Kenya, where state institutions had miserably failed to provide security. These women took initiative and developed a civil society peace building capacity to address that cycle of violence. They initially engaged the elders of different clans, set up a mediation process, and included formal authorities such as the district commissioner. In 1995, the Wajir Peace and Development Committee was established, which broadened participation in the province to include additional government officials, security personnel, religious leaders, NGO representatives, tribal chiefs, and peace advocates. This civil society committee not only brought peace to the Wajir district, but was also used as a model for all districts throughout northern Kenya.

Notably, the districts of Kenya that had such Wajir-like civil society peace committees in place during the aftermath of the December 2007 elections reported far less violence than the districts without such committees.

The CCP, formed on 31 December 2007, immediately drew upon existing civil society peace building capacity and provided a crucial space/avenue for all people to utilize. The CCP's initial focus was to plead publicly and privately with political leaders and candidates to dialogue, while simultaneously reaching out to all Kenyans. In its very first media appearance, the CCP appealed to all Kenyans to halt the violence and called for calm, peace, and dialogue throughout the country. The CCP leaders invited anyone and everyone interested in peace to come to their location, the Serena Hotel, to join the group.

An Open Forum was born, then, on 1 January 2008. The Open Forum's daily morning sessions became the meeting place for civil society group leaders, politicians, private sector representatives, various professionals, the media, and people from all walks of life. Working committees were developed in the areas of Humanitarian Response, Media, Community Mobilization, Resource Mobilization, and High Level Dialogue. Committee members harvested ideas and suggestions from the people gathered at the Open Forum, developed discussions on those topics, and then produced focused actions. The High Level Dialogue committee soon interfaced with a parallel, formal mediation effort led by former UN Secretary-General Kofi Annan.

Besides the working committees, a web of interrelated groups emerged from the Open Forum: the "Concerned Youth for Peace," "Concerned Kenyan Writers," "Concerned Artists and Celebrities for Peace," "Concerned Women," and several others. Each of these groups and their leaders were deliberately linked to other networks/leaders. The resulting interactions encompassed and connected multiple sectors and multiple levels of Kenyan society.

On 9 January 2008, in just 10 days time, the CCP released a document entitled "Citizens' Agenda for Peace." This document provided a 7-point agenda for ending the crisis. Among its points were the building of trust and confidence between the (competing) political parties, closure to the elections, and the formation of a government of national unity. On 28 February 2008, the formal mediation process led by Mr. Kofi Annan (and involving the African Union's Panel of Eminent Personalities) produced its own "National Peace and Reconciliation Accord" – which bore a striking resemblance to the CCP document released weeks earlier.

Recommendation.

1. Stability operations practitioners should consider building "civil society peace building capacity" in states/provinces prone to conflict. Kenya's Wajir Peace and Development Committee – which included women, government officials, security personnel, clan/tribal leaders, religious leaders, NGO representatives, and peace advocates – can serve as a useful model for some fragile states/provinces.

2. In conditions of emergent/spiraling violence in fragile states, it is important for respected leaders – internal and external – to take prompt action to mobilize peace building efforts. In the case of Kenya, the efforts of Ms. Dekha Abdi and the other four leaders of CCP, and the parallel activities of Mr. Kofi Annan and the African Union's Panel of Eminent Personalities, were absolutely critical in grabbing the attention of the Kenyan people and in mobilizing multiple sectors of society for peace building.

3. In conditions of emergent/spiraling violence in fragile states, it is likewise essential that a space/avenue be provided to the people to vent their frustrations and to develop alternatives to violence. In the case of Kenya, the CCP afforded that necessary space/avenue for positive civil society actions.

4. In peace building and conflict resolution actions, those leading the actions should employ an inclusive strategy – one of maximum participation/ representation and transparency. The CCP's call for anyone and everyone to participate, the daily Open Forum, and the active participation of media in the Open Forum, all serve as an excellent example of an inclusive strategy and the resulting benefits.

5. In peace building and conflict resolution actions, those leading the actions should ensure that participation is extended to multiple levels and multiple sectors of society. In the case of Kenya's Open Forum, the "reach" generated by linking the various committees and groups to one another bridged the lines of party, tribe, ethnicity, religion, age, and gender.

Implications.

1. If civil society capacity for conflict resolution is not developed in fragile states, and if respected leaders do not step up in a crisis to use this capacity and to mobilize society for peace building, then conflict can quickly spiral out of control and turn the state into lawless chaos.

2. The need to get the word out to all countrymen to end rising violence and to join peace building efforts (in times of crisis) implies that mass communication venues/resources are readily available. If they are not, peace building leaders should exhaust all available alternatives in order to maximize information dissemination.

Event Description.

This observation is based on the article "Inspiring Citizens' Initiative for Peacebuilding in Kenya," by Paul van Tongeren, New Routes, Volume 15, 4 November 2010.

Comments.

A related article, which also documents the origins of the CCP and its work during the violent aftermath of the December 2007 Kenyan elections, is "Citizens in Action: Making Peace in the Post-Conflict Election Crisis in Kenya," by George Wachira, with Thomas Arendshorst and Simon M. Charles, NPI-Africa and GPPAC, January 2010, found at: http://www.npi-africa.org/publications

Return to
"Quick Look"

f. TOPIC. Enabling Transition in Liberia through Civil-Military Coordination (773)

Observation.

With an eye toward transition, the United Nations Mission in Liberia (UNMIL) shifted the role of the UN peacekeeping force (the UNMIL Force) in early 2008 from "leading" the delivery of services (security, reconstruction, social services, etc.) to "enabling" the Government of Liberia to take lead. The primary measures used by the UNMIL Force in this "enabling" approach were: encouraging all external players to help the host nation (HN) take lead, inserting civilian agencies and HN officials into the approval process and into the full life cycle for all projects and services, and conducting comprehensive information operations to improve the public's perception of the HN government.

Discussion.

In January 2008, the UNMIL Force substantially changed its approach to business after recognizing that the Government of Liberia was becoming increasingly dependent on the Force to deliver services to the public. This increasing dependence was contradictory to the Government of Liberia's own Poverty Reduction Strategy (PRS) – a strategy which had the support of the international community. Through the PRS, the Government of Liberia was supposed to gain the capacity and assume control – particularly at the county level – for the delivery of essential public services, including security, governance, rule of law, and economic and social development. Besides the increasing dependence on the UNMIL Force for service delivery, another assessed problem and threat to civil stability was: large concentrations of idle and unemployed youths.

The UNMIL Force, therefore, in January 2008, changed its approach from "leading" delivery of services and reconstruction projects to "enabling" others – especially the HN government – to assume control of them. The UNMIL Force steadily positioned itself into an indirect role – more clearly in support of the civilian agencies. Instead of planning and leading services/projects, the UNMIL Force instead encouraged coordination and collaboration between the UNMIL's civil component, UN agencies, and NGOs on these services/projects. It further encouraged them to collaboratively put the Government of Liberia in the lead of these activities. A central goal of the UNMIL Force was to work itself out of a job.

Deliberate actions were taken to ensure that civilian partners were inserted and operating between the UNMIL Force and HN entities – at all levels. At the county level, the UNMIL's Joint County Offices (civilian offices) became the conduits for UNMIL Force assistance to HN county administrators/offices. At the national level, the Offices of the Special Representative of the Secretary General (SRSG) and Deputy SRSGs took lead for all civil-military coordination (CIMIC) with HN government agencies/officials. All requests for military support were now "civilianized" – i.e., being processed by a civilian office. To facilitate full transition, ownership, and sustainability by the host nation, all reconstruction projects began to involve Government of Liberia officials. The UNMIL Force front-loaded HN ownership in the assessment phase of reconstruction and social service projects, and it pushed and tracked HN ownership through the planning, coordination, and execution phases. For infrastructure projects facilitated by the UNMIL Force's Quick Impact Project (QIP) program – such as the construction of police stations, courthouses, and detention facilities – local contractors were increasingly selected to execute these projects over the UNMIL Force's own engineer units. This allowed HN civilians to take control and created significant opportunities for local employment.

Success toward transition was also achieved through forging a close relationship between CIMIC and information operations (IO). When development projects were ongoing and measurable progress achieved, corresponding IO messages were developed and delivered. The intent was to shape public perception – that these development projects enhanced future stability and security for Liberians, even if the UNMIL Force was drawing down. This message conveyed that HN assets would be able to sustain these projects and services. To strengthen this message, the UNMIL Fore would put Liberians visibly in the lead at project/service sites. The UNMIL Force would visibly involve HN military and police on all CIMIC projects – transferring the public trust gained by the UNMIL Force to the Government of Liberia. This was especially important for rural areas not being reached by news media. Here it was much more effective to visibly involve local leaders/opinion-makers in the physical execution of projects. Furthermore, the UNMIL Force took steps to bring HN personnel (military and police) into UN CIMIC courses (including instruction on assessments and project management) – further contributing to HN capacity-building and transition.

Significant progress was made by the UNMIL Force in Liberia since 2008 through the utilization of the "enabling" approach – across the various sectors of stability operations. In the security sector, the UNMIL Force was able to instill in the Armed Forces of Liberia (AFL) an ethos of public service and sensitivity to civil society through a number of civil action projects, joint workshops with civil society organizations, and leadership seminars on security-related issues. In the economic stabilization sector, the UNMIL Force was able to provide vocational skills training to over 8,000 ex-combatants and youths, ran agricultural training model farms for thousands more, and supported the Liberian Ministry of Public Works in its management of road rehabilitation projects. In the justice sector, the UNMIL Force helped build local capacity through joint execution of numerous Quick Impact Projects and through oversight of contractors' work on others. Finally, in the social welfare sector, the UNMIL Force was able to provide "on the job" training of Liberian medical personnel during medical outreach programs, as well as to mentor schoolteachers during education assistance programs.

Recommendation.

1. During peacekeeping and stability operations, it is recommended that military forces/peacekeepers conduct civil-military coordination with an eye on transition and an "enabling" approach – "civilianizing" military assistance and building the capacity of the HN government to deliver essential public services.

2. It is recommended that civil-military coordination activities be closely tied to information operations – to build positive public perceptions of the HN govern-

ment and public confidence in the government's ability to provide/sustain security and other essential services.

3. It is recommended that civil-military coordination activities extend beyond capacity-building and information operations: CIMIC should place HN government officials and institutions "visibly" in the lead of service delivery and reconstruction efforts – in public/open forums – to further expand/strengthen public trust and confidence in the HN government.

Implications.

If military forces/peacekeepers do not have an eye on transition from the outset of peacekeeping and stability operations, and if they do not have a strong "information operations and confidence-building campaign" to contribute to transition, then they could find themselves playing "catch-up" when drawdown/ redeployment approaches. Also, the HN government might fall short on capacity to sustain the delivery of essential public services. Negative public opinion could result, which could lead to renewed instability.

Event Description.

This observation is based on the article "Civil-Military Coordination and Transition Management: The UNMIL Experience," by Christopher Holshek in Conflict Trends, Issue 3, 2011.

g. TOPIC. **Disengagement Strategy in Kandahar, Afghanistan** (1259)

Observation.

The Kandahar City-District Stabilization Team (KC-DST), in close coordination with Combined Task Force (CTF) Lancer, reversed the trend of "excessive International Security Assistance Force (ISAF) support to Kandahar City officials" and implemented a new strategy (disengagement strategy) to put "Afghans in the lead." As a result, the host nation/municipal government is now on course toward sustainable self-sufficiency.

Discussion.

In May 2012, the newly arrived leadership (civilian and military) of the KC-DST conducted a comprehensive review of the KC-DST's operations, with the determination that its personnel were not adequately placing "Afghans in the lead" with regard to governance. Over the past several years, the standard way of doing business with city officials essentially consisted of KC-DST/ISAF personnel, as well as ISAF/donor funding, being involved in virtually all development projects and service deliveries across the city.

The KC-DST is a 31-person civilian and military team focused on the development of Kandahar City governance. The civilian members of this team (11 total) consist of the following personnel: two Department of State (DoS) officers, four United States Agency for International Development (USAID) officers, one USAID Office of Transition Initiatives (OTI) officer, and four Foreign Service Nationals (FSNs). The military component of the KC-DST is a Security Force Assistance Team (SFAT) made up of 20 personnel: four Army officer advisors and a 16-soldier Security Force (SECFOR). The KC-DST's mission is: to increase the outreach, capacity, transparency, and legitimacy of the municipal government with specific focus in all these areas toward transition to sustainable self-sufficiency.

However, the KC-DST's April 2012 operational review revealed that although many projects and municipal services were successfully ongoing in the city, the vast majority were ISAF/donor funded. Furthermore, these projects and services were typically being financed at exorbitant rates, meaning that contractors would reject lower-paying municipal projects because they knew they could gain more lucrative contracts funded by ISAF/donors. These over-priced contracts undermined Kandahar City's budget planning/programming/execution efforts.

According to the KC-DST's April 2012 review, another major impediment to Afghan self-sufficiency was ISAF's excessive mentoring of Afghan officials. All interactions among Afghans affecting the municipality – whether among personnel within the same municipal office, or between the municipality and provincial offices, national ministries, businesses, and other external actors – were being coordinated, orchestrated, moderated, and tracked by (previous and current) members of the KC-DST/ISAF. Although well-intentioned, this practice left Afghan municipal officials completely dependent upon the KC-DST/ISAF to handle even the simplest issues/requirements/actions.

To address the Kandahar City budget planning/programming/execution problem, the KC-DST coordinated with CTF Lancer (the ISAF task force operating in Kandahar) to cooperatively end ISAF's funding of expiring and new municipal infrastructure projects. In response to this ISAF funding drawdown, the Kandahar City government took some initiative and established a "municipal response fund for urgent requirements." Since the inception of this fund, the municipality has tapped into this internal resource numerous times for emerging infrastructure requirements – all completely independent of ISAF involvement. Also, rather than pay exorbitant prices for outside engineers to develop cost estimates for projects, the mayor of Kandahar (1) hired ten high school graduates and arranged for them to be trained as engineering technicians and (2) received national-level funding to hire an additional ten employees/technicians above the standard pay-scale. Most importantly, ISAF's withdrawal of funding soon led to an increase in contractors' bidding on standard-rate municipal projects, since there were no ISAF-funded projects/contracts on the horizon. Because of these factors/changes, the Kandahar City government has thus far been able to execute a 2013 budget 2½ times larger than the previous year, and it has developed a multi-year list of projects that will drive future budget planning/ programming/execution.

To reverse the other trend of excessive KC-DST/ISAF mentorship, the KC-DST leadership implemented a strict new policy of limiting mentoring activities down to discussion/advice with only the individual who raises a given issue/requirement/ action. The advice given by KC-DST personnel now only consists of suggesting which parties/stakeholders the Afghan official should engage with – to develop an "Afghan" course of action/solution. The CD-DST now no longer sets up meetings, moderates discussions, or tracks the issues through resolution – which has allowed Kandahar City officials to assume ownership of resolving their own municipal problems, generated much greater Afghan-to-Afghan cooperation/ communication, and quickly built up Afghan governance capacity for Kandahar City.

Recommendation.

1. The KC-DST's "disengagement strategy" should be replicated in other municipalities and provinces across Afghanistan, in the interest of having all government offices on a course of sustainable self-sufficiency.

2. Stabilization and reconstruction efforts should place restrictions/stipulations on all donor-funded projects, as follows: (a) host nation ownership is instituted upfront during project formulation, (b) host nation resources are applied/invested in the project from the outset, and (c) time limits are set to gradually drawdown the external funding, allowing the host nation budgeting process to incorporate and sustain projects over time.

3. Intervening forces/actors should set (short-term) timelines for the reduction of mentorship activities, allowing host nation officials to take ownership of issues, agendas, meetings, coordination, issue tracking, issue resolution, etc. as early as possible.

Implication.

Unless a disengagement strategy is developed and implemented at an early stage of stability operations – one that establishes timelines on donor-funded projects and external mentorship activities – resources will be wasted because of over-priced contracts, and host nation officials will remain dependent upon the intervening forces/officials/donors for too long a time.

Event Description.

This lesson is based on the article "Disengagement: A Strategy that Works; Kandahar City's Change of Course Toward Sustainable Self-Sufficiency," by COL Cordell Fox, U.S. Army, in COIN Common Sense, Volume 4, Issue 2, April 2013.

Comments.

Related references:

(1) Enabling Transition in Liberia through Civil-Military Coordination, David Mosinski, SOLLIMS Lesson 773, 23 November 2011.

(2) Strategic Lesson Number 10: The "Essentials" of Transition, Dan French and David Mosinski, PKSOI, 11 July 2012.

(3) Status of Developing Afghan Governance and Lessons for Future Endeavors, Steven Sternlieb, *Stability: International Journal of Security & Development*, 2(1): 12, pp. 1-10, DOI: http://dx.doi.org/10.5334/sta.ay, 9 May 2013.

(4) Afghanistan: Meeting the Real World Challenges of Transition, Anthony H. Cordesman, Center for Strategic & International Studies (CSIS), 23 January 2013.

(5) Creating Voids: Western Military Downscaling and Afghanistan's Transformation Phase, Florian P. Kuhn, The Centre for International Governance Innovation (CIGI), 16 January 2013.

Return to
"Quick Look"

h. **TOPIC.** Civilian Casualty Tracking in Afghanistan (**1256**)

Observation.

During Operation Enduring Freedom (OEF) in Afghanistan, the tracking and analysis of civilian casualties, along with command emphasis on civilian casualty (CIVCAS) prevention, led to a significant decrease in civilian casualties – positively impacting attitudes in the host nation toward the International Security and Assistance Force (ISAF) and host nation security forces.

Discussion.

In late 2008, General McKiernan, the ISAF Commander in Afghanistan, established the first Civilian Casualty Tracking Cell (CCTC) in ISAF – to better enable his commanders and staff to monitor harm to civilians. In mid-2009, as leaders grew to realize that civilian casualties were in fact adversely impacting the stability mission, the next ISAF Commander, General McChrystal issued a Tactical Directive (6 July 2009) that stated:

> "We must avoid the trap of winning tactical victories – but suffering strategic defeats – by causing civilian casualties or excessive damage and thus alienating the people.... I expect leaders at all levels to scrutinize and limit the use of force like close air support (CAS) against residential compounds and other locations likely to produce civilian casualties.... The use of air-to-ground munitions and indirect fires against residential compounds is only authorized under very limited and prescribed conditions." [Headquarters, ISAF, 6 July 2009]

After gathering data for several months, the CCTC was then able to identify/ assess CIVCAS trends over time. Based on those assessments, the ISAF Commander developed and issued additional guidance to the force – adjusting ISAF's tactics and procedures in order to further decrease harm to civilians. For example, when data began to show that Afghan civilians were being killed in numerous traffic accidents caused by ISAF forces/drivers, the ISAF Commander issued a directive on driving (30 August 2009), which instructed soldiers to avoid aggressive driving and to instead emphasize safe driving. Likewise, when night raids were found to be contributory to Afghan casualties as well as cause for great irritation/anger among host nation citizens, the ISAF Commander issued a directive on night raids (5 March 2010), which directed commanders/units to explore all other feasible options before conducting any night raid in the vicinity of compounds and residences. That directive further stated the following:

> "The ISAF policy on Night Raids builds upon earlier directives which establish guidance on entry into Afghan medical facilities to respect and protect innocent civilians; on driving, instructing ISAF personnel to adhere to appropriate, legal driving procedures and behavior in Afghanistan; and, an over-arching Tactical Directive which provides guidance and intent for the employment of force in support of ISAF operations by gaining and maintaining the support of the people, by separating the insurgency from the innocents, and by avoiding civilian casualties through the application of an appropriate use of force." [Headquarters, ISAF, 5 March 2010]

Subsequent ISAF commanders continued to place strong emphasis on CIVCAS prevention. For example, General Petraeus modified the Tactical Directive (4 August 2010) to more effectively protect civilians across the range of situations where they could be involved. General Allen likewise issued his Tactical Directive (30 November 2011) – calling for an even more judicious application of force, soldier discipline, tactical patience, and regular reinforcement training – guided by Rules of Engagement (ROE). An OEF CIVCAS Smart Card and an

OEF CIVCAS Handbook were also produced to facilitate awareness and education across the force. In conjunction with these directives and supplements, the CCTC provided the comprehensive data and trend analysis that informed ISAF commanders. That analysis enabled commanders to make informed decisions and to adjust tactics and procedures as needed.

The results speak for themselves. Civilian casualty rates dropped significantly over a 4-year timeframe. According to the United Nations Assistance Mission in Afghanistan (UNAMA), 828 civilians had been killed by pro-government forces (ISAF and host nation security forces) in 2008. One year later, in 2009 (Note: the CCTC was stood up in late 2008 and General McChrystal's Tactical Directive was issued in July 2009), the number of civilian casualties caused by pro-government forces dropped to 596. By 2012, the number of civilian casualties caused by pro-government forces was down to 316. Overall, through tracking, analysis, and recognition of how much civilian harm was occurring and its causes, ISAF commanders were able to adapt and make a positive impact on both CIVCAS reduction and host nation attitudes.

Recommendation.

1. Forces involved in peacekeeping and stability operations should establish a Civilian Casualty Tracking Cell (CCTC) [also referred to as a Civilian Casualty Tracking, Analysis, and Response Cell (CCTARC)] – to provide commanders with accurate CIVCAS information and analysis of trends. Commanders should ensure that this cell is adequately staffed, resourced, and trained.

2. Commanders should emphasize the importance of Protection of Civilians (PoC) and CIVCAS prevention to all soldiers throughout peacekeeping/stability operations, providing clear guidance on tactics and procedures.

Implication.

If CIVCAS is not tracked and analyzed by a dedicated cell, then commanders may not be able to conduct informed decision-making on this critical issue. Additionally, if commanders do not continuously emphasize CIVCAS prevention to their troops, then civilian casualties may rise, and host nation attitudes toward the international force may worsen – to the detriment of the overall campaign.

Event Description.

This lesson is based on the article "Operationalizing Civilian Protection in Mali: The Case for a Civilian Casualty Tracking, Analysis, and Response Cell," by Marla B. Kennan, 11 June 2013. Keenan, M.B. 2013. Operationalizing Civilian Protection in Mali: The Case for a Civilian Casualty Tracking, Analysis, and Response Cell. *Stability: International Journal of Security and Development* 2(2):21, DOI: http://dx.doi.org/10.5334/sta.ba

Comments.

Related references:

(1) ATTP 3-37.31 Civilian Casualty Mitigation, Headquarters, Department of the Army, July 2012.

(2) Protection of Civilians Military Reference Guide, Dwight Raymond, Bill Flavin, and Juergen Prandtner, PKSOI, January 2013.

(3) SOLLIMS Sampler – Protection of Civilians, Dan French and David Mosinski, PKSOI, 2 January 2013.

(4) Strategic Lesson Number 13: The Imperative of Protecting Civilians, Dan French and David Mosinski, PKSOI, 27 November 2012.

(5) Afghanistan Annual Report 2008 – Protection of Civilians in Armed Conflict, UNAMA, January 2009.

(6) Afghanistan Annual Report 2012 – Protection of Civilians in Armed Conflict, UNAMA, February 2013.

(7) Progress Toward Security and Stability in Afghanistan, Department of Defense, July 2013.

Return to "Quick Look"

3. CONCLUSION

Over the course of recent peacekeeping and stability operations, a number of "key enablers" have significantly contributed to mission accomplishment. What follows is a recap of the "key enablers" identified in this publication – along with recommendations for future operations.

(1) "Information-gathering and analysis" mechanisms.

(a) Establish robust "information gathering and analysis" mechanisms – focused on the population – to provide forces/commanders of peacekeeping and stability operations with a comprehensive understanding of the operating environment.

(b) Information collected at the ground level – from patrols, CA teams, force protection teams, MIST teams, human terrain teams, reconstruction teams, key leader engagements, etc. – should be given the greatest attention in peacekeeping and stability operations/environments. The preponderance of information and intelligence resources should be focused at this level, with sufficient analysts deployed at this level to manage PIR, IR, collection activities, de-briefings, analysis, and dissemination. Although "tactical" in nature, this information is absolutely vital to the production of accurate "operational" and "strategic" intelligence.

(2) Civ-mil planning teams.

    (a) Within any given U.S. embassy, establish and empower a planning team (like CMPASS) to focus on ensuring that the strategic plan is followed. This team could help facilitate periodic assessments to measure progress on the goals set forth in the strategic plan and propose courses of action to address gaps or deficiencies. This team could also facilitate periodic civ-mil "Rehearsal of Concept" (ROC) drills to enhance stakeholder collaboration.

    (b) Those involved in the complex business of planning stability operations should come to recognize the critical importance of building personal relationships. Planning is likely to improve when civilians and service members take time to get to know one another, understand the constraints others are working under, and learn what is motivating them to work on the plan/operation.

(3) Strategic messaging / information operations.

    (a) Continue to utilize MISO in support of stability operations – to help influence the attitudes/behaviors of the local populace in support of U.S./coalition operations, and to affect/impact the decision-making of opposition leaders/groups/supporters.

    (b) Combatant Commanders should request MISO and Commando Solo assets early on during crisis/contingency planning – and incorporate these personnel into appropriate staffs/teams such as the Joint Planning Team, Targeting Cell, and Humanitarian Working Group.

(4) Police units with policewomen.

    (a) The UN should continue the approach of sending all-female FPUs on select peacekeeping operations. This should be done on a case-by-case basis, depending on the UN's assessment of the given host nation environment and the willingness of contributing countries to deploy such units. In certain environments, all-female FPUs may be able to serve as key role models for host nation women and girls.

    (b) The UN and other organizations/coalitions engaged in peacekeeping operations should consider the benefits of having their deployed police/security forces engage in community "peace building" programs and activities.

(5) "Peace building" programs.

    (a) Consider building "civil society peace building capacity" in states/provinces prone to conflict. Kenya's Wajir Peace and Development Committee – which included women, government officials, security personnel, clan/tribal leaders, religious leaders, NGO representatives, and peace advocates – can serve as a useful model for some fragile states/provinces.

    (b) Employ an _inclusive_ strategy – one of maximum participation/representation and transparency. Kenya's creation of a "central" civil society organization, the call for anyone and everyone to participate, the holding of a daily "open forum," and the continuous involvement of the media were key elements of an inclusive strategy that quickly produced positive results.

(6) Governance capacity-building strategies.

    (a) Military forces/peacekeepers should develop governance capacity-building strategies that "civilianize" military assistance and build the capacity of the HN government to deliver essential public services. Excellent examples are: (1) UNMIL's "enabling" approach in Liberia and (2) KC-DST's "disengagement" strategy in Kandahar, Afghanistan.

    (b) As part of the governance capacity-building strategies, HN government officials and institutions must be placed "visibly" in the lead of service deliveries and reconstruction projects – through public/open forums and media releases – to strengthen the public's trust and confidence in the HN government, thereby building legitimacy.

    (c) Intervening forces should set (short-term) timelines for the reduction of mentorship activities, allowing HN officials to take ownership of issues, agendas, meetings, coordination, issue tracking, issue resolution, etc. – as early as possible.

    (d) Intervening leaders/actors should place restrictions/stipulations on all donor-funded projects, as follows: (1) HN ownership is instituted upfront during project formulation, (2) HN resources are applied/invested in the project from the outset, and (3) time limits are set to gradually draw down the external funding, allowing the HN budgeting process to incorporate and sustain projects over time.

(7) CIVCAS prevention measures.

    (a) Forces involved in peacekeeping and stability operations should establish a Civilian Casualty Tracking Cell (CCTC) or Civilian Casualty Tracking, Analysis, and Response Cell (CCTARC) – to provide commanders with accurate CIVCAS information and analysis of trends. Commanders should ensure that this cell is adequately staffed, resourced, and trained.

    (b) Commanders should emphasize the importance of Protection of Civilians (PoC) and CIVCAS prevention to all soldiers throughout peacekeeping/stability operations, providing clear guidance on tactics and procedures.

Through wider dissemination of the aforementioned "enablers" and associated recommendations, their inclusion in planning events, and leadership emphasis, efficiencies may be gained on future peacekeeping and stability operations.

4. <u>COMMAND POC</u>

Lessons selected by: Mr. David Mosinski, PKSOI Lessons Learned Analyst.

PKSOI reviewer: Mr. Dan French, Chief, Lessons Learned Branch.

Contact information:
    Email: <u>usarmy.carlisle.awc.mbx.sollims@mail.mil</u>
    Phone: (717) 245-3031
    DSN: 242-3031

# RELATED DOCUMENTS, REFERENCES, AND LINKS

- "Strategic Lessons in Peacekeeping & Stability Operations, Vol. 1 (Summer 2012)," Dan French and David Mosinski, PKSOI, 31 July 2012

- "Strategic Lessons in Peacekeeping & Stability Operations, Vol. 2 (Summer 2013)," Dan French and David Mosinski, PKSOI, 2 August 2013

- "Lessons Learned from UN Operations" folder / documents in SOLLIMS shared library

- "Stabilisation & Reconstruction: Definitions, Civilian Contribution & Lessons Learnt," Civil Military Fusion Centre (CFC), September 2011

- "Decade of War, Volume I: Enduring Lessons from the Past Decade of Operations," Joint and Coalition Analysis (JCOA), Joint Staff J7, 15 June 2012

- "Newsletter 10-12: Multinational Operations," Center for Army Lessons Learned (CALL), December 2009

- "Guiding Principles for Stabilization and Reconstruction," United States Institute of Peace (USIP) and PKSOI, October 2009

- "Guide for Participants in Peace, Stability, and Relief Operations," United States Institute of Peace (USIP), 2007

- "SOLLIMS Sampler – Protection of Civilians," Vol. 4, Issue 1," Dan French and David Mosinski, PKSOI, 2 January 2013

- "SOLLIMS Sampler – Civ-Mil Cooperation, Vol. 3, Issue 2," Dan French and David Mosinski, PKSOI, 3 April 2012

- "Integrating Peace Building with Peace & Stability Operations", Franco Gacal, SOLLIMS Lesson 1147, 23 November 2011.

U.S. Army Peacekeeping and Stability Operations Institute (PKSOI)	
Director	COL Jody Petery
Chief, Operations	COL Robert Balcavage
Chief, Lessons Learned Branch	Dan French
Lessons Learned Analyst	David Mosinski